THE RAVEN.

Once upon a midnight dreary,
While I pondered, weak and weary,
Over many a quaint and curious
Volume of forgotten lore—
While I nodded, nearly napping,
Suddenly there came a tapping,
As of some one gently rapping,
Rapping at my chamber door.
"'T is some visitor," I muttered,
"Tapping at my chamber door—
Only this and nothing more.

Ah, distinctly I remember
It was in the bleak December,
And each separate dying ember
Wrought its ghost upon the floor.
Eagerly I wished the morrow;—
Vainly I had sought to borrow
From my books surcease of sorrow—
Sorrow for the lost Lenore—
For the rare and radiant maiden
Whom the angels name Lenore—
Nameless here for evermore.

And the silken sad uncertain
Rustling of each purple curtain
Thrilled me—filled me with fantastic
Terrors never felt before ;
So that now, to still the beating
Of my heart, I stood repeating,
" 'T is some visitor entreating
Entrance at my chamber door—
Some late visitor entreating
Entrance at my chamber door ;
This it is and nothing more."

Presently my soul grew stronger ;
Hesitating then no longer,
" Sir," said I, " or Madam, truly
Your forgiveness I implore ;
But the fact is I was napping,
And so gently you came rapping,
And so faintly you came tapping,
Tapping at my chamber door,
That I scarce was sure I heard you "—
Here I opened wide the door :——
Darkness there and nothing more.

Deep into that darkness peering,
Long I stood there wondering, fearing,
Doubting, dreaming dreams no mortals
Ever dared to dream before ;
But the silence was unbroken,
And the stillness gave no token,

And the only word there spoken
   Was the whispered word, " Lenore ! "
This I whispered, and an echo
   Murmured back the word, " Lenore ! "—
      Merely this and nothing more.

Back into the chamber turning,
All my soul within me burning,
Soon again I heard a tapping
   Something louder than before.
" Surely," said I, "surely that is
Something at my window lattice ;
Let me see, then what thereat is,
   And this mystery explore—
Let my heart be still a moment
   And this mystery explore ;—
      'T is the wind and nothing more."

Open here I flung the shutter,
When, with many a flirt and flutter,
In there stepped a stately Raven
   Of the saintly days of yore.
Not the least obeisance made he ;
Not a minute stopped or stayed he ;
But with mien of lord or lady,
   Perched above my chamber door—
Perched upon a bust of Pallas
   Just above my chamber door—
      Perched, and sat, and nothing more.

Then this ebony bird beguiling
My sad fancy into smiling,
By the grave and stern decorum
Of the countenance it wore,
"Though thy crest be shorn and shaven,
Thou," I said, "art sure no craven,
Ghastly grim and ancient Raven
Wandering from the Nightly shore—
Tell me what thy lordly name is
On the Night's Plutonian shore!"
Quoth the Raven, "Nevermore."

Much I marvelled this ungainly
Fowl to hear discourse so plainly,
Though its answer little meaning—
Little relevancy bore;
For we cannot help agreeing
That no living human being
Ever yet was blest with seeing
Bird above his chamber door—
Bird or beast upon the sculptured
Bust above his chamber door,
With such name as "Nevermore."

But the Raven, sitting lonely
On that placid bust, spoke only
That one word, as if his soul in
That one word he did outpour.
Nothing farther then he uttered;
Not a feather then he fluttered—

Till I scarcely more than muttered,
"Other friends have flown before—
On the morrow *he* will leave me,
As my Hopes have flown before."
Then the bird said, "Nevermore."

Startled at the stillness broken
By reply so aptly spoken,
"Doubtless," said I, "what it utters
Is its only stock and store,
Caught from some unhappy master
Whom unmerciful Disaster
Followed fast and followed faster
Till his songs one burden bore—
Till the dirges of his Hope that
Melancholy burden bore
Of 'Never—nevermore.'"

But the Raven still beguiling
All my sad soul into smiling,
Straight I wheeled a cushioned seat in
Front of bird, and bust and door ;
Then upon the velvet sinking,
I betook myself to linking
Fancy unto fancy, thinking
What this ominous bird of yore—
What this grim, ungainly, ghastly,
Gaunt and ominous bird of yore
Meant in croaking "Nevermore."

This I sat engaged in guessing,
But no syllable expressing
To the fowl whose fiery eyes now
Burned into my bosom's core ;
This and more I sat divining,
With my head at ease reclining
On the cushion's velvet lining
That the lamplight gloated o'er,
But whose velvet violet lining,
With the lamplight gloating o'er,
She shall press, ah, nevermore !

Then methought the air grew denser,
Perfumed from an unseen censer
Swung by Seraphim, whose footfalls
Tinkled on the tufted floor.
" Wretch," I cried, " thy God hath lent thee—
By these angels he hath sent thee
Respite—respite and nepenthe
From thy memories of Lenore !
Quaff, oh quaff this kind nepenthe,
And forget this lost Lenore ! "
Quoth the Raven, " Nevermore."

" Prophet ! " said I, " thing of evil !—
Prophet still, if bird or devil !—
Whether Tempter sent, or whether
Tempest tossed thee here ashore,
Desolate, yet all undaunted,
On this desert land enchanted—

On this home by Horror haunted—
Tell me truly, I implore—
Is there—*is* there balm in Gilead?
Tell me—tell me, I implore!"
Quoth the Raven, "Nevermore."

"Prophet!" said I, "thing of evil—
Prophet still, if bird or devil!
By that Heaven that bends above us—
By that God we both adore—
Tell this soul with sorrow laden
If, within the distant Aidenn,
It shall clasp a sainted maiden
Whom the angels name Lenore—
Clasp a rare and radiant maiden
Whom the angels name Lenore."
Quoth the Raven, "Nevermore."

"Be that word our sign of parting,
Bird or fiend," I shrieked, upstarting—
"Get thee back into the tempest
And the Night's Plutonian shore!
Leave no black plume as a token
Of that lie thy soul hath spoken!
Leave my loneliness unbroken!—
Quit the bust above my door!
Take thy beak from out my heart, and
Take thy form from off my door!"
Quoth the Raven, "Nevermore."

The Raven.

And the Raven, never flitting,
Still is sitting, still is sitting
On the pallid bust of Pallas
Just above my chamber door ;
And his eyes have all the seeming
Of a demon's that is dreaming,
And the lamplight o'er him streaming
Throws his shadow on the floor ;
And my soul, from out that shadow
That lies floating on the floor,
Shall be lifted—nevermore !

—EDGAR ALLAN POE.

LUCY GRAY.

Oft I had heard of Lucy Gray:
And, when I crossed the wild,
I chanced to see at break of day
The solitary child.

No mate, no comrade Lucy knew;
She dwelt on a wide moor,
—The sweetest thing that ever grew
Beside a human door!

You yet may spy the fawn at play,
The hare upon the green;
But the sweet face of Lucy Gray
Will never more be seen.

"To-night will be a stormy night—
You to the town must go;
And take a lantern, Child, to light
Your mother through the snow."

"That, Father, will I gladly do!
'T is scarcely afternoon—
The minster-clock has just struck two,
And yonder is the moon."

Lucy Gray.

At this the Father raised his hook
  And snapped a faggot band ;
He plied his work ;—and Lucy took
  The lantern in her hand.

Not blither is the mountain roe :
  With many a wanton stroke
Her feet disperse the powdery snow,
  That rises up like smoke.

The storm came on before its time :
  She wandered up and down ;
And many a hill did Lucy climb ;
  But never reached the town.

The wretched parents all that night
  Went shouting far and wide ;
But there was neither sound nor sight
  To serve them for a guide.

At day-break on a hill they stood
  That overlooked the moor ;
And thence they saw the bridge of wood,
  A furlong from their door.

And, turning homeward, now they cried,
" In heaven we all shall meet ! "
—When in the snow the mother spied
  The print of Lucy's feet.

Lucy Gray.

Then downward from the steep hill's edge
  They tracked the footmarks small ;
And through the broken hawthorn hedge,
  And by the long stone wall :

And then an open field they crossed ;
  The marks were still the same ;
They tracked them on, nor ever lost ;
  And to the bridge they came.

They followed from the snowy bank
  The footmarks, one by one,
Into the middle of the plank ;
  And further there were none !

—Yet some maintain that to this day
  She is a living child ;
That you may see sweet Lucy Gray
  Upon the lonesome wild.

O'er rough and smooth she trips along,
  And never looks behind ;
And sings a solitary song
  That whistles in the wind.

—William Wordsworth.

www.ingramcontent.com/pod-product-compliance
Lightning Source LLC
LaVergne TN
LVHW020643110826
845149LV00004B/1333

* 9 7 8 1 4 1 8 1 8 9 4 8 8 *